Walt Whitman

by Sheila Griffin Llanas

Content Consultant
Adam Bradford, PhD

CORE
LIBRARY

Published by ABDO Publishing Company, PO Box 398166, Minneapolis, MN 55439. Copyright © 2013 by Abdo Consulting Group, Inc. International copyrights reserved in all countries. No part of this book may be reproduced in any form without written permission from the publisher. The Core Library™ is a trademark and logo of ABDO Publishing Company.

Printed in the United States of America,
North Mankato, Minnesota
112012
012013

Editor: Kari Cornell
Series Designer: Becky Daum

Cataloging-in-Publication Data
Llanas, Sheila Griffin.
  Walt Whitman / Sheila Griffin Llanas.
    p. cm. -- (Great American authors)
  Includes bibliographical references and index.
  ISBN 978-1-61783-720-3
  1. Whitman, Walt, 1819-1892--Juvenile literature. 2. Poets, American--19th century--Biography--Juvenile literature.   I. Title.
  811/.3--dc23
  [B]
                                            2012946818

Photo Credits: Bettmann/Corbis/AP Images, cover, 1, 4, 7, 34, 45; Library of Congress, 9, 18, 21, 32, 38, 40; Picture History, 10; Red Line Editorial, 12, 30; Library of Congress, 15; Private Collection/The Bridgeman Art Library, 16; North Wind/North Wind Picture Archives, 24, 27, 36; Jacquelyn Martin/AP Images, 28, 43

CONTENTS

CHAPTER ONE
A Life-Changing Journey   4

CHAPTER TWO
Home on Long Island   10

CHAPTER THREE
Leaves of Grass   16

CHAPTER FOUR
A Civil War Volunteer Nurse   24

CHAPTER FIVE
After the War   32

CHAPTER SIX
Growing Older   38

Important Dates 42
Key Works 43
Stop and Think 44
Glossary 46
Learn More 47
Index 48
About the Author 48

A Life-Changing Journey

On the night of April 13, 1861, Walt Whitman attended an opera in New York City. Afterward he strolled down to lower Manhattan. He wanted to catch the ferry home to Brooklyn. Before he reached the port, a crowd had formed. Newsboys sold newspapers on the streets. Whitman bought one. Under a streetlamp, he read the news. The American Civil War had started.

The First Battle of Bull Run inspired Walt Whitman to write his famous poem "Beat! Beat! Drums!"

Drum-Taps

Whitman's poems about the Civil War express the emotional state of the nation. As a hospital wound-dresser, he saw the sadness of war. His poems grew somber. After the war ended and President Abraham Lincoln died, Whitman published *Drum-Taps* in 1865. Later he added *Drum-Taps* as a section in *Leaves of Grass*. The war poems in *Drum-Taps* capture Whitman's firsthand account of an important time in US history. They present a picture of the Civil War from beginning to end.

Five months later, after the First Battle of Bull Run, Whitman wrote these lines: "Beat! beat! drums!—Blow! bugles! blow! Over the traffic of cities—over the rumble of wheels in the streets . . ."

Whitman's poem expressed what many Americans felt. War filled daily life. Like many, Whitman thought the war would only last a few months. He had yet to see the battlefields where soldiers fought.

At 42 years old, Whitman was too old to fight. He stayed in New York to care for his mother. He visited wounded soldiers in the Broadway Hospital to

In his poems about the war, Whitman captured the beat of typical fife and drum corps, such as this one, shown at a Civil War camp.

cheer them up. As a journalist, he wrote many articles. About the Broadway Hospital, he wrote, "What a tragic poem there is in every one of those sick wards!"

The Search for His Brother

Whitman's brother, George Whitman, joined the Union army. Eager for war news, Whitman read George's letters and the daily newspapers. One day in December 1862, Whitman opened the *New York Herald*. He read the list of soldiers killed or wounded in action. One name stood out. A First Lieutenant

G. W. Whitmore was wounded at the Battle of Fredericksburg. George fought at Fredericksburg. The name was so close. Perhaps it was misspelled. Whitman believed his brother was hurt.

Wasting no time, Whitman boarded a train to Virginia. The train stopped in Washington DC. While Whitman waited for his next train, a thief stole his wallet. With no money, he was stuck in the nation's

EXPLORE ONLINE

The focus of Chapter One is the start of the Civil War. It also touches on Whitman's search for his brother. The Web site below focuses on Whitman's poems written during the Civil War era. As you know, every source is different. How is the information given on the Web site different from the information in this chapter? What can you learn from this Web site?

Walt Whitman and *Leaves of Grass*

www.loc.gov/exhibits/treasures/whitman-poetofthenation.html

This image of a young Whitman in the early 1850s appeared on the first page of the *Walt Whitman Fellowship Papers*, published in 1895–1896.

capital. Whitman searched the city's hospitals. He was determined to find his brother—or his brother's grave.

CHAPTER TWO

Home on Long Island

Walt Whitman was born on May 31, 1819. He was the second child of Walter and Louisa Whitman. The Whitmans lived on a 500-acre (200-ha) farm on Long Island, New York. Walter was a farmer and a carpenter, but he struggled to earn money. On May 27, 1823, the Whitmans moved 20 miles (32 km) away to Brooklyn. Walter built and sold houses to support his family.

The Whitman family lived in this house in West Hills, New York, when Walt Whitman was born.

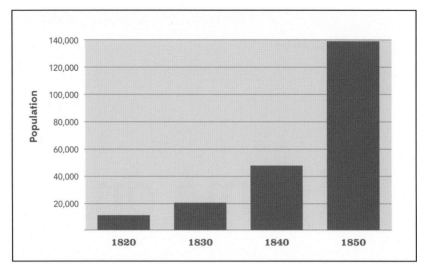

From Town to City, Brooklyn's Growth in Walt Whitman's Time

Whitman moved to Brooklyn in 1824. Brooklyn was small in the 1820s. What happened to the population in Brooklyn over the decades? How old was Whitman in 1850? What changes do you think he saw during that time?

Even as a young person, Walt liked to dream. He loved to ride the Fulton Ferry from Brooklyn to Manhattan. He made friends with the ferrymen. He watched the horses that powered the ferry. For the rest of his life, he had a passion for ferries.

Finding His Calling

Walt left school at age 11. He needed to earn money to help support his family. He got a job in a law office.

One of the lawyers urged Walt to practice his reading and writing. Walt read Homer, Dante, Shakespeare, and the Bible.

In 1833 Walt's parents returned to the family farm. Walt remained in the city. He was 14 years old. He became an apprentice for a newspaper called the *Long Island Patriot*. He learned to set type. At that time, books were printed on a printing press. Each letter of every word was set in a row. It was like writing with small alphabet blocks. Walt's new job nurtured his love of writing. Unlike his father, who worked with his hands, Walt wanted to work with words.

Meeting a General

In 1824 five-year-old Walt saw General Lafayette, an aid to George Washington in the American Revolution. The general visited Brooklyn to celebrate the town's first public library. People guided schoolchildren through the crowd. Lafayette helped. He lifted Walt and set him down in a safe place. This was one of Walt's favorite stories. He told it often throughout his life.

Early Short Stories

Before Walt became a poet, he wrote fiction. These three early short stories have moral lessons that reflect his life and beliefs:

- "Death in the Schoolroom"
  A strict teacher beats a student for something he did not do.
- "Wild Frank's Return"
  A boy runs away from his father. When he returns, he is killed by a horse.
- "Bervance"
  A boy is sent to an insane asylum by his father. The boy escapes, leaving home for good.

A Journalist

In 1835 Walt began to work for a printer in Manhattan. In his spare time, he went to the theater. He joined debate clubs. On December 16 tragedy struck. The Great Fire of 1835 burned 50 acres (20 ha). Many businesses were ruined. The economy came to a halt.

Walt went home to Long Island. At age 17, he became a teacher to help his struggling family. Although Walt was popular with his students, school board members did not think Walt was strict enough. They did not renew his contract.

The Great Fire of 1835 blazed through the city of New York on December 16 and 17, killing 20 people and destroying the city's financial center.

At age 19, Walt bought his own printing press. He started a newspaper called the *Long Islander*. He delivered the first issue on horseback on June 5, 1838. A year later, he sold the press and moved back to Manhattan.

Walt never held a job for long. In 1846 Walt worked for the *Brooklyn Daily Eagle*. For almost ten more years, Walt worked as a journalist and editor for newspapers. Then his life changed once more.

CHAPTER THREE

Leaves of Grass

Whitman enjoyed being a journalist. He wrote about his interests. He crafted a writing style that expressed his spirit. In his free time, he strolled through Brooklyn or Manhattan. He attended the theater, opera, lectures, and art exhibits. He spent hours in libraries. He filled his editorials and news articles with the sights and sounds of city life.

This engraving of Whitman, created in 1855, appeared on the first page of Leaves of Grass.

Whitman used common language when writing about his day-to-day experiences.

To others Whitman did not appear successful. He turned down offers for steady jobs. Instead he worked odd jobs. No one understood his intellect.

Whitman appeared idle. However, he was always busy thinking. He believed he could express the ideas of a nation. He believed that art helped people—and nations—become strong and free.

Whitman felt a growing desire to write poetry. From 1850 to 1855, Whitman wrote poems that changed American poetry forever.

Themes

Whitman filled his poetry with important themes. He praised democracy and humanity. He used nature and music to describe life, birth, and death. Whitman wrote his poems as if they were songs. He felt connected with all of humanity. He wanted to speak for everyone.

Whitman had a unique and bold writing style. He used common words. He did not want his poems to be scholarly. He wrote in free verse, meaning he did not use

Whitman's Siblings

Whitman was very close to his seven siblings. His siblings were older brother Jesse and younger siblings Mary Elizabeth, Hannah Louisa, Andrew Jackson, George Washington, Thomas Jefferson, and Edward. Jesse and Edward were both mentally impaired. Walter Sr. and Louisa named three sons after well-known politicians. Little did they know it would be Walt who would go down in history.

rhyme or meter. He often wrote long lists of images in his poems. The descriptions made his poems expansive and joyful.

Leaves of Grass

In June 1855, Whitman hired a Brooklyn print shop to print 1,000 copies of his book of 12 long poems. Whitman set some of the type himself.

Leaves of Grass went on sale on July 6, 1855. Whitman wrote three reviews himself to stir interest. Even so, few people bought or read the book.

Two Important Readers

Ralph Waldo Emerson wrote to Whitman personally, praising *Leaves of Grass*. Whitman was thrilled with this letter. He carried it in his pocket for months.

Whitman's other admirer was a man few people knew yet. Abraham Lincoln kept a copy of *Leaves of Grass* on a table in his law office.

The approval of Ralph Waldo Emerson, a great American thinker and writer, meant the world to Whitman.

A Second and Third Edition

In 1856 Whitman printed a second edition of *Leaves of Grass*. Inside he printed Emerson's letter. The second edition sold less than the first. Whitman worked on his poems for the rest of his life. He revised and expanded the book.

In 1859 a Boston publisher asked to publish the third edition. Whitman went to Boston to help

Befriending Omnibus Drivers

Whitman loved to ride New York City omnibuses, large horse-drawn stagecoaches. He knew the drivers by name. For hours he would sit up front, listening to the drivers tell "yarns," or stories. Once a driver fell ill. Whitman took the man's route until he grew well again. He gave the wages to the driver's family.

produce the book. It had grown to 456 pages, with 146 new poems. This time between 2,000 and 5,000 copies were printed. This edition sold more than the earlier printings.

When Ralph Waldo Emerson read *Leaves of Grass*, he sent Walt Whitman a personal letter of praise. This well-known letter has been widely reprinted.

> *Concord, Massachusetts, 21 July, 1855*
>
> *Dear Sir,*
>
> *I am not blind to the worth of the wonderful gift of "Leaves of Grass." I find it the most extraordinary piece of wit & wisdom that America has yet contributed. . . . It meets the demand I am always making of what seemed the sterile & stingy Nature, as if too much handiwork or too much lymph in the temperament were making our western wits fat & mean.*
>
> *. . .*
>
> *I greet you at the beginning of a great career. . . . I rubbed my eyes a little to see if this sunbeam were no illusion. . . . It has the best merits, namely, of fortifying & encouraging.*
>
> *. . .*
>
> *R. W. Emerson*
>
> Source: Walt Whitman. Leaves of Grass. 1856. Ed. David S. Reynolds. New York: Oxford, 2005. Print. 161.

Back It Up

Write a paragraph describing Emerson's main point. Then write down two or three pieces of evidence Emerson uses to make his point.

CHAPTER FOUR

A Civil War Volunteer Nurse

When the American Civil War began, Whitman was in New York, far from the fighting. He read all the newspapers. He based his high-spirited war poems on the news he read. He was about to get a firsthand look at the battlefields.

Whitman worked alongside nurses such as this one in Civil War hospitals. He befriended Union and Confederate soldiers, fed them meals, and helped them write letters home.

A Civil War Copyist

During and after the Civil War, Whitman worked as a government copyist. He handwrote documents about topics such as the trial of Jefferson Davis and railroad expansion. Today there are 3,000 documents in Whitman's handwriting. These documents are historical artifacts. They are stored in the National Archives in Washington DC.

The Search for George

In December 1862, Whitman was stranded in Washington DC with no money. He searched the war hospitals for his brother. He walked day and night in confusion through crowds. He could not find his brother. Whitman found a friend working a wartime government job. The friend gave him money and a military pass. Whitman took a train to Virginia. On December 19, 1862, in Falmouth, Virginia, he found George at last. In a battle that killed many soldiers, George had only a minor cut.

For a week and a half, Whitman ate and slept in the camp. He saw soldiers who were homesick,

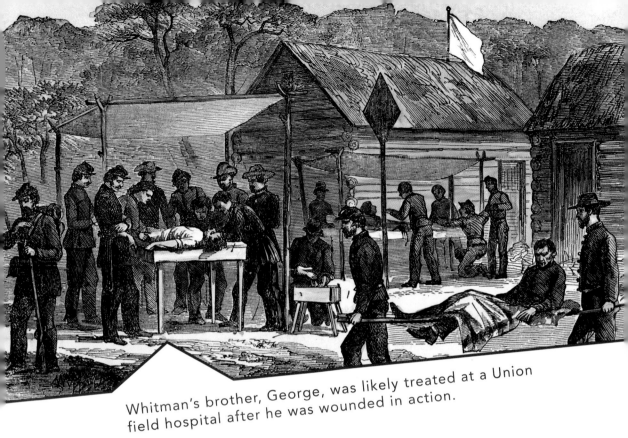

Whitman's brother, George, was likely treated at a Union field hospital after he was wounded in action.

hungry, and exhausted. He saw injuries and deaths, horrors that shocked him. Whitman returned to Washington DC. He planned to stay one week. He remained there for the rest of the war.

Serving as a Wound-Dresser

Whitman became a Civil War volunteer nurse. He lived in a boardinghouse. In his free time, he visited wounded Union and Confederate soldiers. He served

...ice. The Attorney Gen...

...atter _ex parte_ at this...

...le to take it up for...

...ou receipt of such...

...marks as the Comm...

...to offer. To that e...

...nsmit them.

Respectfully, Your ...

M. F. ...

Chie...

Thousands of documents penned by Whitman are stored in the National Archives in Washington DC.

suppers, talked with the soldiers, and helped them write letters home. He treated minor injuries. He sat with patients during surgeries and sleepless nights. He wanted to lift their spirits. Whitman often visited Armory Square, where the worst cases were treated.

He carried small notebooks and wrote about what he saw. He filled his poems with images of war hospitals. He wrote articles for New York newspapers and firsthand accounts of the war. They were read by people eager for news, as he had once been.

Letters Home

Whitman did important work for dying soldiers. He wrote sympathy letters to their parents. He consoled the families of soldiers who died. He wanted parents to remember their sons with love and pride. He described the soldier's last days, reporting what the soldier said and how he looked. "Rest assured that your son died in a noble cause," he wrote to a father and mother. After the war, some soldiers wrote to Whitman, thanking him for his friendship.

Civil War Soldiers	Enlisted	Died of Injury or Disease
Union army	2,000,000 plus	360,000
Confederate army	1,000,000 plus	260,000

Civil War Hospitals in Washington DC	Location	Number of Beds or Cots
Lincoln General	15 blocks east of the Capitol	2,575
Capitol Building	1500 Pennsylvania Avenue	2,000
Armory Square	National Mall	1,000

Civil War Deaths and Hospitals

During the Civil War, 85 hospitals were set up in Washington DC. Three of the largest hospitals are listed above. Beds were placed in churches, warehouses, schools, and museums. How important was Whitman's role as a volunteer nurse? What parts of his job were easy or hard? What challenges did he most likely face every day?

Near the war's end, Whitman counted that he had nursed more than 80,000 soldiers. So many soldiers had suffered and died. Many had no family or friends. Though he tried to stay optimistic, Whitman grew depressed. He slept badly. Images of wounded and dying soldiers stayed in his mind for the rest of his life.

Excerpt from "I Hear America Singing" by Walt Whitman

I hear America singing, the varied carols I hear,
Those of mechanics, each one singing his as it should be
blithe and strong,
The carpenter singing his as he measures his plank or
beam,

. . .

The boatman singing what belongs to him in his boat, the
deckhand
   singing on the steamboat deck,
The shoemaker singing as he sits on his bench, the hatter
singing as he stands,

. . .

Each singing what belongs to him or her and to none else,
The day what belongs to the day—at night the party of
young fellows,
   robust, friendly,
Singing with open mouths their strong melodious songs.

Source: Walt Whitman. Leaves of Grass. 1860. New York: Modern Library, 1921.
Print. 9–10.

What's the Big Idea?

Read the poem carefully. Why did Whitman describe workers as singing? Write down the main idea of this poem. Use examples from the poem to support your ideas.

CHAPTER FIVE

After the War

In April 1865, Whitman took time off from his job in Washington DC. He went to New York to publish *Drum-Taps*, his collection of poems about the war. Again he paid for the book himself.

His early war poems had the sound of brass drums, glory, and pride. In the rhythm of marching soldiers, he wrote "Beat! Beat! Drums!" Later poems described the costs of war. He described the pain he

Whitman, age 71, poses for a studio photograph against a nature background.

Wake up & see the ~~shining sun~~, & see the
flags a-flying; ~~??~~ *splendid sun*.
For you it is the Cities ~~want~~ *about?* - for you the
shores are crowded;
For you the *red-rose* ~~rosy~~ garlands, and ~~the many~~ *electric* eye
of women;
O Captain! O my father! my arm I ~~place~~ *push*
around you;
It is ~~some~~ Dream that on the ~~Deck~~
Yo~~u~~ *slumber, pale*

Whitman wrote the words "O Captain! O my brother!" on this sheet of paper when he learned of President Lincoln's death.

saw. He could never forget the soldiers who became
his friends. So many soldiers died. In his poem "Vigil
Strange I Kept on the Field One Night," he wrote
about a soldier who stayed all night with a friend who
had died on the battlefield.

On April 9, the Civil War ended. On April 14,
1865, President Abraham Lincoln was shot and killed.
Whitman was in Brooklyn, visiting his mother. He read
the news over breakfast. He was stunned and grief-
stricken. He wrote a poem about his sadness called

"O Captain! My Captain!" In the fall of 1865, Whitman printed another elegy to President Lincoln called "When Lilacs Last in the Dooryard Bloom'd."

After the war, Whitman did not return to the spirited poetry he used to write. He still lived in Washington DC. He kept his government job and wrote poems. At 50 years old, Whitman had long white hair, making him look older than he was. To an outsider, he appeared poor. He gave a lot of his money away, however, to

Seeing President Lincoln

Whitman lived near the home and office of Abraham Lincoln in Washington DC. He saw the president almost every day. On August 12, 1863, Whitman wrote in his journal: "Mr. Lincoln on the saddle generally rides a good-sized, easy-going gray horse, is dress'd in plain black, somewhat rusty and dusty, wears a black stiff hat, and looks about as ordinary in attire, etc., as the commonest man. . . . I see very plainly Abraham Lincoln's dark brown face, with the deep-cut lines, the eyes, always to me with a deep latent sadness in the expression."

President Lincoln rides on horseback alongside General Hooker as they check in on the Union army of the Potomac during the Civil War.

his family and friends. He visited Brooklyn often to see his family.

Health Problems

Although Whitman cared for his health, he began to feel weak and dizzy. Doctors believed the war years took a toll on his health, both physically and mentally. He was neither as strong nor as happy as he used to be.

One day he cut his thumb badly. In the late 1800s, even a small cut could be a problem. Infection could lead to gangrene. Whitman went home to Brooklyn to

FURTHER EVIDENCE

There is quite a bit of information in Chapter Five about Walt Whitman and how he changed after the Civil War. If you could pick out the main point of the chapter, what would it be? Visit the Web site below to learn more about Whitman's poems. Choose a quote from the Web site and write a few sentences explaining how it relates to the chapter.

Walt Whitman's Poems

www.poetryfoundation.org/poem/174748

heal. He returned to his job in Washington DC, but he still was not in strong health.

One night in January 1873, Whitman walked home from his office through a cold rain. In the middle of the night, he woke. He could not move his left arm and leg. He did not know it, but he had suffered a stroke. It left him paralyzed.

CHAPTER SIX

Growing Older

The year of 1873 was bad for Whitman. In May his mother grew ill. He was with her when she died on May 23. It was the darkest day of Whitman's life.

Then he lost his government job. Friends worried Whitman might not recover from so much bad luck.

Walt Whitman sits with his nurse, Warren Fritzinger, near the wharf in Camden, New Jersey.

Whitman lived in this house on Mickle Street in Camden, New Jersey, for the last 20 years of his life.

A Poet's Work

The next phase of Whitman's life was as exciting as the first. He gave lectures on President Lincoln. He recited the poems he wrote for Lincoln. Audiences were eager to hear stories of the famous president.

In 1881 a Philadelphia publisher printed the seventh edition of *Leaves of Grass*. This time 1,000 copies sold out in a month. At age 63, Whitman began writing a book called *Specimen Days*. He still wrote poems.

The Cottage in Camden

After his mother died, Whitman stayed in New Jersey. With money from his books and lectures, he bought a house on Mickle Street in 1884. Friends and fans visited him. Some took pity on the way he lived. His small house was cluttered with papers. Whitman, as he always did, appeared to lack money.

He left one final version of *Leaves of Grass* in 1891. Sometimes called the Deathbed edition, the last edition has 389 poems and is 438 pages long. When Whitman died on March 26, 1892, mourners waited in line to pass his coffin. Since his burial in Harleigh Cemetery in Camden, visitors have continued to pay their respects to the great American poet.

Historic Sites Today

Whitman's birthplace in West Hills, Long Island, is now a historic site. The Walt Whitman Birthplace Association was created in 1949. The house, built by Whitman's father in 1810, has been restored.

In the last years of his life, Whitman paid for the plot, planned the design, and hired workers to build his tomb. The tomb is marked only with his name: Walt Whitman. It is surrounded by trees. Many people visit Whitman's house and grave.

IMPORTANT DATES

1819
Walt Whitman is born in Long Island, New York, on May 31.

1823
The Whitman family moves to Brooklyn on May 27.

1835
The Great Fire of 1835 destroys part of New York City. Whitman returns to Long Island.

1855
The first edition of *Leaves of Grass* is sold on July 6.

1862
Whitman finds his brother, George, on December 19.

1865
President Abraham Lincoln is assassinated on April 14. Whitman begins his tribute to the president.

1873
Whitman suffers a stroke and is partially paralyzed.

1873
Whitman's mother, Louisa, dies at age 80 on May 23.

1884
Whitman purchases a house in Camden, New Jersey.

1891
Whitman issues *Leaves of Grass*, the final edition.

1892
Whitman dies on March 26.

KEY WORKS

Leaves of Grass

Walt Whitman's groundbreaking volume of poems had 12 poems in 1855. His final edition, in 1891, was 438 pages long and had 389 poems.

Whitman, Walt. *Leaves of Grass*. Brooklyn, 1855. Print.

Specimen Days and Collect

Walt Whitman collected the stories and memories of his life, beginning with his childhood on Long Island, New York.

Whitman, Walt. *Specimen Days and Collect*. Philadelphia: Rees Welsh and Company, 1882. Print.

Attorney General, fin... the ...parte at this stage, will be ...ake it up for consideration ...ceipt of such statements or ...ks as the Commissioner may th... ...o offer. To that end I herewith ...smit them.
Respectfully, Your obedient servant
M. F. Pleasants,
Chief Clerk.

Why Do I Care?

Walt Whitman's childhood was very important to him. In what ways was his childhood like yours? In what ways was it different? He saw changes in the world as he grew up. What changes in the world have you seen?

You Are There

Walt Whitman loved the street life in Brooklyn, New York. Imagine that you live in Brooklyn in the 1830s. It is a small farming community. Put yourself in Whitman's shoes. What would you see on your walk through Brooklyn to catch the Fulton Ferry to Manhattan? In 300 words, describe the sights, smells, and sounds you would experience along the way.

Tell the Tale

For much of Walt Whitman's life, he did not know how important his poetry would become. In 200 words, explain why he is so important. What was different about his poetry? How did the changes in the United States during his time affect his writing?

Take a Stand

Walt Whitman quit school to work at age 11. Take a position on education and jobs for children and teenagers. Write a short essay detailing your opinion. Be sure to give reasons for your opinion and support those reasons with facts and details.

GLOSSARY

apprentice
someone who learns a skill by working with an experienced worker

blithe
joyous, carefree, light-hearted

edition
version

editor
a person who revises and corrects a text

editorial
an article that states an opinion on a topic, not just information

elegy
a poem written for someone who has died

expansive
big, far-seeing

gangrene
an illness that kills body tissue

intellect
the mind; intelligence

melodious
having a melody; sweet sounding and musical

optimistic
expecting the best; positive

scholarly
educated; learned from books

somber
a feeling that is gloomy and serious

LEARN MORE

Books

Hollander, John, ed. *American Poetry*. New York: Sterling, 2004.

Kerley, Barbara. *Walt Whitman: Words for America*. Illus. Brian Selznick. New York: Scholastic, 2004.

Levin, Jonathan, ed. *Walt Whitman*. New York: Sterling, 2004.

Web Links

To learn more about Walt Whitman, visit ABDO Publishing Company online at **www.abdopublishing.com**. Web sites about Walt Whitman are featured on our Book Links page. These links are routinely monitored and updated to provide the most current information available.

Visit **www.mycorelibrary.com** for free additional tools for teachers and students.

INDEX

American Civil War, 5–7, 25–30, 34

Armory Square, 29, 30

"Bervance," 14

Brooklyn Daily Eagle, 15

"Death in the Schoolroom," 14

Drum-Taps, 6, 33

Emerson, Ralph Waldo, 20–21, 23

First Battle of Bull Run, 6

free verse poetry, 19–20

Great Fire of 1835, 14

Harleigh Cemetery, 41

"I Hear America Singing," 31

illness, 36–37, 39

Lafayette, General, 13

Leaves of Grass, 6, 20–22, 40, 41

Lincoln, Abraham, 6, 20, 34–35, 40

Long Island, New York, 11, 14, 41

Long Island Patriot, 13

Long Islander, 15

National Archives, 26

New York Herald, 7

printing press, 13, 15

soldiers, 6, 26–27, 29, 30, 33–34

Specimen Days, 40

themes, 19–20

Walt Whitman Birthplace Association, 41

Washington DC, 8, 26–27, 30, 33, 35, 37

Whitman, George, 7–8, 19, 26

Whitman, Louisa, 11, 19, 39, 40

Whitman, Walter, 11, 13, 19, 41

"Wild Frank's Return," 14

writing style, 17, 19–20

ABOUT THE AUTHOR

Sheila Griffin Llanas is a poet and author. She writes informational books for children on many topics. She lives in Milwaukee, Wisconsin, with her husband and their dog.